Nuthouse Romance
and other prose

Nicklaus Barnes

BookLeaf Publishing

India | USA | UK

Presentation by *BookLeaf Publishing*

Web: www.bookleafpub.com

E-mail: info@bookleafpub.com

ISBN: 9789360941604

First edition 2024

I dedicate this book to all the people I've met in my journey who are still out there, trying to make do in a world that despises us. May you and they find peace and contentment.

ACKNOWLEDGEMENT

I'd like to thank my best friend Cori for always encouraging me, my friend Mondo for pointing me in the right direction, my aunt for being there when I needed her most, and my brother for being my north star.

PREFACE

This eclectic collection of writing merges prose and short stories to allow you to feel the tale, not just hear it. My hope is that reading this book will allow the reader to feel compassion and empathy for those who are struggling in ways the reader may not have ever experienced.

Preamble

We the people of the United States
Except for the Poor behind the locked gates
In order to form a more perfect Union
Old crooks, new crooks, neither have a solution
Establish Justice insure Domestic Tranquility
With a Police state ran by the Homeland
Security
Provide for the common Defense
War is good in a Business Sense
Secure the blessings of Liberty
It helps if you're a Celebrity
For ourselves and our Posterity
Excluding Social Security
Do ordain and establish this Constitution
Now, a deteriorating Resolution
For the United States of America
Faded to be a Restricted Area

Automaton

</start>
I am a cyborg of sorts,
a composition of
Insults, Neglect,
Pity and Possibilities

an amalgamation of
Tragedies
and Privileges
I may or may not
be aware of

equal parts shit-talk
and exaltation

held together
with a thin bead of
humor and deflection
scotch-taped with witticisms
a threadbare string
of jests
tied together with a quip
and only banter
to back me up

because I prefer to
receive my Trauma
without all of the
associated Drama

Loading…

a PTSD virus
ravaged my programming;
when I tried to hug
my step-mother
as a kid,
"get your
Dick-Skinners
off me"
her words
would bid

echoing
in my head as
they carved a grisly
and mocking
smile into the
yielding flesh
of my forearm

ERROR

my survival

was hailed,
Miraculous!
and
Meaningful!
reigniting the
lost Potential
that had been
snuffed out
by my Addiction.

rebooted

and the
brainwashing
by christofascists
in their version
of "rehab"
attempted to take root
In my subprograms

lean not
on your own
understanding,
but in all your ways,
do what we say,
if heroin
didn't break you,
conversion therapy
may.

reset to factory settings?

their trojan horse
called jesus
burned through
my software
and corrupted
my hard drive
but was overwritten
by the queer code
that underpins
my entire
programming.

reset complete

</end>

Nuthouse Romance

There you were, standing there, rail thin, the last place you wanted to be, the last place I wanted to be and you walk with a radiance that exuded your desire to be left alone, ignore me, don't notice me, how could I not notice you, not be drawn to you and you went straight to your room and I didn't see you again till meal time when you ate no more then three bites of food and I attempted to talk to you but you gave me a cold stare that said I don't have a clue what your going through, beat it, but I knew exactly what you were going through, because it takes one to know one, both at our rock bottoms grasping for the light at end of the cell and I notice the next day you didn't even come to breakfast so I went to you and asked how you were doing and you said to me dope sick how do you think and I said not good, I just finished kicking myself, it gets better, then they gave a med call and when they gave me my two Norco's and ativan because the powers that be had deemed me worthy of their use, I stuck them under my tongue and swallowed the rest of my pills and went back to your room and said "hey these have been in my mouth but I think you need them more than me

and by the way my name is Nick" and you
jumped up and grabbed them up and swallowed
them then looked me in the eyes and smiled
saying "thank you" and it was the first time I
saw that smile, the most beautiful thing I had
seen since my journey through the center of the
psych ward had begun and worth more than the
tingle I would have got from the pills, and that
evening as I sat and watched the news you came
in to the rec room and pulled a chair up next to
me and wrapped a blanket around yourself as
you wrapped your hand around mine and the
news was irrelevant as you told me the story of
how your boyfriend sold Oxy to pay for your
apartment and you smoked ten 80's on the daily,
but try as you might, you could never catch that
dragon no matter how long you chased him, how
he was cheating on you and dumped you (your
boyfriend not the dragon) and with one fell
swoop your love and your supply was gone so
you thought you'd see how long it would take to
hit the ground after jumping off the forest hill
bridge, but when you got out there the
emergency phone they have for just such
occasions made you think twice, you used it and
the operator had you picked up by a cop, the last
thing a junkie wants, who took you to our
present place of residence and I told you the
same story, but a knife instead of a bridge,

heroin instead of Oxy, then they told us we
couldn't hold hands, no romantic relationships
were to be had in the nuthouse and by the way
it's lights out, go to bed so we did but I awoke to
you shaking me telling me you were sad and
sick and scared and so sorry for waking me but
you couldn't sleep and you were lonely and
could I lay down and just hold you so you could
feel safe and I said yes, so we snuck back into
her room and I lay next to you and kissed your
forehead and told you I was there and it was
okay, just go to sleep and it felt so pure and real
compared to the reality we had been in and I
knew if I was caught I would be reprimanded
but I wasn't in their because I followed rules so I
lay there and you slept in my arms and I thought
about staying there forever until I got an urgent
premonition to get out so I peeked out the door
and they were going room to room taking blood
samples, so as they went into one room I snuck
back into mine, them none the wiser, and we
spent the next day together until your ex came to
visit and I wanted to smash him for causing you
pain but I didn't want to get booty-juiced then
strapped down naked in the rubber room and
miss out on any moments that could be spent
with you, so instead I sat with you in your room
afterwards and put my arm around your shoulder
and the nurse saw and freaked out, so you told

her that I was comforting you, you wanted me
there and they said that's the psychiatrists job,
don't let us catch you in their again or vice versa
and we laughed thinking about what they would
have done if they had caught me comforting you
the night before and we went to arts and crafts
were you made me a bracelet with black star
beads, blue rose beads and a single black and
blue heart, confessing that was how your heart
was, all bruised and beaten and I told you that it
was punk rock, I love it, wishing instead I had
said "I love you" and the next day I was
scheduled to be released so you gave me your
phone number hugged me and held my hand
saying that I was what made your time their
bearable and it felt like we had been friends for
5 years not 5 days and I told you to get off the
stuff and that you are beautiful and deserve
better than your ex and then you kissed me and
our lips touched for only a few seconds in front
of everyone but what could they do to punish us
now that was worse than having to say goodbye,
and your face was framed in that little window
in the door like a portrait from the 1600's
because your smile was gone and I lost my
wallet that I had kept your number in, making
that the last time I saw my psych ward partner,
my nuthouse romance.

The Most Patient Thing I Know

It always seems to be there
lurking beneath the surface.
people don't see it
my friends and family
can't hear it approaching
and I don't feel it
all the time

but when I get
a little angry
a little lonely
a little tired
a little depressed
when I'm bored out of my mind
and think it's totally dead
it whispers to me
you can do it just once
no one will know
you're doing so well
you deserve to celebrate

it disguises itself
as a potential mate
a job promotion

a sudden influx of cash
it entices me
lies to me
tries to shove me off my path

it tells me it wants me to have it all
but it takes it all away

it tells me to have fun
but gives me pain and suffering

it tells me to enjoy my life
as it tries to kill me

it tells me it knows who I am
as it makes me into what I'm not

it tells me that I'm free
then secures me in my bondage

it tells me it's my best friend
when it's really my greatest adversary

Midnight at Noon

the pain
is instantly
overshadowed
with joy
as the black caddy
delivers to the
asphalt pharmacy
the temporary vaccine
to my affliction

the sickly sweet scent
of the tarry substance
fills my nostrils
sending a
pavlovian tingle
of anticipation
down my spine

ash smears
my hands as,
shakingly,
i draw the
antidote
to my despair

to 75 cc's

as the black
rubber tip of
the plunger sinks
further down
it grows until
my vision is filled
and I fall
headfirst
into the darkness

Staring at Profile Pictures

Though
    it's been
        ages

Everytime
    I open
        my profile

I still hope
    that I find
        a message

        from
        you.

It doesn't matter why

It doesn't matter why you took your first drug
Whether your mother never gave you a hug
Or you just wanted to be a thug
At first you were able to sweep it under the rug

But then you realize you're just another poor sap
Caught in the trap
It's a wrap

Because addiction
Doesn't ask permission
For its infliction
Of the degradation
In your situation
For filling you with pollution
Or for sticking you into an institution
But there is a solution

When you're at the end of your rope
Just trying to cope
And say nope
To dope
We have a hope

And after where we've been

Leading lives of sin
In the pits of the devil's den
We all need to say Amen

Freeform

A Blank sheet of paper
you have so much potential
The beginning of a masterpiece
a work of origami
cut and put into a scrapbook

You're versatile
after all
you've come a long way
A tree in some forest
peaceful, serene
Then taken from the womb
crushed, torn, shredded,
separated from the rest

Some became a house,
or a boat
or furniture
Not you
The leftovers
made into a wet pulp
pressed together
into anorexic sheets

Sent to OfficeMax

or Staples
You've traveled far
Will it be worth it?

Or will you end up
a crumpled ball
thrown into the trash
spit wad ammo
a paper airplane
that dive bombs after 3 feet

From forest to failure
and wilderness to wonder
Whatever you end up being
it is what you were meant to become

Disorderly conduct

Escaping disorderly conduct
                         Everyday espionage
Disenfranchised strangers
                                pleading
        "Please save me!"

The best friends
        I ever had
            still want
                something
      from me.

Love poem #1

I wanted to write you a love poem
That wasn't cheesy or cliche
Love seems to be a poet's favorite topic
Yeah it's the hardest thing to capture

How to express the inexpressible?
To try and put it into words
It's like seeing a lion in the zoo
It shouldn't be confined to the page

Like describing music to a deaf person
Some things have to be experienced to
understand

It's like a photo of a sunset
Still beautiful
But nothing can compare
To the real thing

Erotic Poem

I love you
Lying there, flat,
Glistening with oil
Hot to the touch
So inviting
Awaking animal lusts
Deep within my core

With a name
So sweet

Bacon!

I look around

We called this the real world
Yet all I see
Is a materialistic masquerade
A superficial shell

All people see are shades of gray
Yet tell each other
Descriptions of majestic hues
Of magenta, burgundy, and neon green
With a touch of black and white
To make it believable

What they need they don't want
What they want only brings death and despair

Their philosophies, morals, religions
Everything they claim to believe,
And matters to them most
Is forgotten the moment the argument ends

Their successes are only temporary
Their failures can't be admitted

Everyone acts like they have it all figured out
When no one has a clue

The people's kind and compassionate Acts
Are made vile by their motivations

Their love is too shallow
It only goes balls deep

They admire the rich and the famous
While hating on the success of their peers

Amidst fanfare, they give to charity
With the same breath, curse the person with the
cardboard sign

They vote at the polls to lower taxes
Then lose their jobs and expect to live off Social
Security

They demand Justice by sending drug addicts to
prison
Whilst drinking their cocktails and taking double
their prescribed dosage

But, worst of all
They judge those around them
Never admitting to
Their own, hypocritical, guilt

Her

She put him out
like a midnight cigarette
Though crushed and broken
the fire burned on

He tore at himself
fingernails ragged
they cut jagged falls
that cascaded from his wrist
splattering the floor
damming up the rivers
with Bic smiley faces

Though all this pain
could not mask
the terminal hurt
that permeated his heart

He drank for a living
because love was his drug
til one day he showed her
his Love's extent
Not with the pencil and paper
songs and poems,
twitter or text

Not by showing up
on her doorstep, unannounced

NO

What he had to say
could not be said
So with a cotton rope
and the snap of his neck
he showed her exactly
what is love, truly, meant

Generation

We like to smoke a bowl
drink whiskey, have sex
Eat shrooms to enhance our soul
or be chased by the pink T-Rex

We live for the weekend
The good times with bad
Say bon voyage to old friends
Only to miss what we had

Leading lives filled with sin
we go to work, parties, and school
The wheel continues to spin
and we still act the fool

Outdated morals, "Do as we say!"
The man's attempts to keep us at bay
And when we are caught not following his way
He puts us in cuffs, and takes us away

yet still we persist
Stubborn no doubt
Until we discover
what life's all about

Nerd Love

I am astounded when I think about it. How could it be? I can't pinpoint one particular reason. It's an enigma. Understanding the complexities of the universe or how the eye works; simple brain teasers and riddles compared to this. It gets me all worked up until...

    ... I remember I don't have to understand it...

    ... I just have to accept it. The fact is you love me. And it means more to me than the complexities of the universe or how the eye works or all the brain teasers and riddles in the world. Combined.

I'll do anything to return the favor.

AM/PM

The automatic doors open and shut
Letting the black booted laborers
With their tools and attitudes
Inside to receive their allotment
Of gasoline and preservatives.
The day's work demands as much
as do the pumps to which they return.
They wheeze sympathy and smog.

Just inside the door
the numbered snake crosses the wall
Seizing up the many marked Intruders.
Perched in the corner
the security eye has them clocked
with a steady digital reckoning.
It never blinks.

Passerby only nod, tight-lipped
At the howling newspaper headlines.
If they could just look up
They might catch themselves and see
It's such a quick stop
to be stuck between
Payday and Milky Way

The florescent aisles
Beckon like the gates of heaven
Angels and advertising
Glaring down at you
Into your soul
Judging, knowing

The cashier accepts your money,
Charon on the river Styx
Framed by tobacco and lottery tickets
The register accepts the offering.

The coughing engine sputters to life
After the long nose of the pump
deposits it's payload
The yellow stripes
On the back of the black, asphalt eel
Leads them back out
Into the night.

Under the Bridge

Wake up to cars driving overhead
Find the last of my pint
then check to make sure
that i'm grubby enough looking
to evoke pity

Walk to the 7/11 to panhandle
Only need $6.05 to purchase
a pint of Barrets, rot gut, whiskey
and a can of coke

Chug them down in three swags
Then back to the 7/11
Only this time i dont need a chaser
and repeat…
Til im drunk enough to float

Walk down to st. vinny's
for my free hot meal
They allow you to take seconds
so i eat up

Then off to the library
Reading, the only thing
that made life worth living

besides intoxicants

Return to my bridge
with Dean Koontz's "Frankenstein"
under my arm
Only to find a friend
with a free shot of crank for me

Now I have to shit
But no public restrooms
So I shit in a plastic bag
then toss it into the bushes
That sack of shit
a fitting metaphor for my life
Spend the whole night
searching for treasures
and recycling
in society's refuse
Like me,
it's lost and unwanted

Then I get paranoid
and believe the cops
are after me
So I squat in a bush
til the early morning

Returning to my nest of
warm blankets and plastic bags

And my life affirming
pint of whiskey

My motto is,
"Don't get drunk, stay drunk."
What else is there to do
when you are homeless?

Attractive Emigma

They say that beauty
is in the eye of the beholder
Society tries to make blonde, thin, curvy
the cookie cutter idea of beauty.
Lust driven anticipations of
"Love 'em and leave 'em"

One night stands
Satisfying our single serving,
ADD masses
But the surface...
If we scratch it we find
Perceptions are not constant
The beholder is not a common denominator

So what is beautiful?

Is it judged as a black or white
Yes or no definite?
On a scale of 1 to 10?

What makes a thing beautiful,
And what makes it ugly?
Are we machines following a pattern
We picked up from our environment?

By inborn knowledge?

Is beauty found in purity
Innocence
Undamaged goods
A baby, a plant
Organized and clean?

Nothing will stay as such for long
Change is uncomfortable
The real beauty is found in the mess
Splendor in the quagmire

Like a sunset
It's most beautiful
when it's polluted with smog
Like real people
imperfect and chaotic
Their flaws define their beauty

Rx: A Haiku

Pharmacuticals
First, they are all fun and games
Then you get strung out

Hotshot

One Sunday morning on the way to the methadone clinic, Barnaby was thinking about getting high. And not just any high. A full-on, hell-bent, till the wheels fall off, bender. They'd been thinking about it for some time now. However, as they had learned in rehab, they were playing the tape forward. First the bliss from that initial high, but it wouldn't stop there. Dependence rides on the tailcoats of euphoria, then it won't leave when the party is over. And then the struggle. Getting drugs, hiding the fact that you are high, getting more drugs, losing your job, home and relationships, and getting more drugs. Finally, you are reduced to a level of junk existence, where everything is dimmed out and barely subsisting, and you submit all of your energy, mind, and soul to the addict's odyssey. Because it's not the drugs that cause the problem, nor is it from resentments as they say in A.A. It comes from the constant wrenching of your psyche from ebullient bliss to the pure, feral desperation that not having drugs produces, and back again.
Barnaby flicks out their cigarette as they walk into the clinic, deciding that, today at least, they

were just going to take their methadone and remain in recovery. They checked in at the front desk and then sat to wait their turn at the dispensing window. As one person would leave, they would hold the door open for the next patient. When it was Barnaby's turn, the previous person in line closed the door before they could walk in. Quizzically, Barnaby looked at them. They shrugged their shoulders and said the nurse had told them to. Barnaby sat back down.

The nurse walked into the waiting room and said, "Unfortunately we have just run out of medication, and our delivery does not arrive till tomorrow. We are sorry for the inconvenience." Panic gripped Barnaby's mind as they realized they had been unable to dose the day before and were already starting to feel dope sick. The fragile foundation they had laid for their recovery was blasted apart like an m-80 in a tin can. They checked their phone, hoping beyond hope that they hadn't deleted every connect's number from it. They had.

"O.k., plan B," they thought, as they walked to their car. They drove to the bad part of town, the part of town that they used to call their stomping grounds, before "Recovery". They had befriended some unhoused folks that lived near the levee and had maintained these relationships, you know, just in case. They walked to the first encampment behind the levee but sadly they didn't recognize any faces.

They began asking around for Mimi, the lady they had bought crank from, from time to time. They had decided that since they were getting high today anyway, they might as way mainline. Unfortunately, they didn't have the knowledge or the courage, to do this to themself, so they were going to need a clean outfit and some crank to give to the local street medic, Boxer. Once inside the trick triage unit, and after paying your tax of a $5 bag of criss, and giving them your rig, you get hit in 3 pokes or less, guaranteed. Sometimes this did include vigorous push-ups and arm-swinging to increase blood flow to certain areas.

After much haggling and waiting on various "friends" of Mimi's to show up and deliver the different drugs and equipment needed for the operation, Barnaby showed up at the door of room 7 upside-down C, at the Sleazy 8 motel, where Boxer had set up operations for the night. Barnaby was as sick as a no-masker with covid-19. It became apparent that Boxer hadn't had any customers that day and was obviously going through withdrawals as well. So Boxer insisted on shooting themself up with the clear sack first so that their "hands wouldn't shake."

They also asked if Barnaby had a spare clean
outfit on them. Barnaby told them that they
didn't. Boxer began setting up a re-sanitation
station for a rig they needed to clean that they
had used once on a previous customer. They set
up two Donald duck dixie cups, one with bleach,
one with water, and began sucking and squirting
the bleach in and out. They pulled the plunger
out, dipped it in the bleach then scrubbed it with
their dirty fingers til they were satisfied they had
killed the possible hiv. They rinsed it all out
then moved the two cups aside to set up their
spoon, into which they dumped the salary sack
of crystal meth. They crushed it with the lid of
the rig, then filled it with a clear liquid from the
Donald dixie cup, searched out a vein, and with
one poke found their blood flag and injected the
whole thing. They pulled the needle from their
flesh and began smacking their lips and said, "
this must be good stuff." Barnaby smiled.
"Woah," Boxer said as they grabbed the edge of
the bathroom counter. Barnaby looked down at
the two dixie cups and with horror leaned their
nose down to Boxer's spoon and took a sniff.
The smell their nose registered was …
BLEACH!
"Oh fuck, dude, fuck, shit, you just gave
yourself a fucking hotshot! Jesus Christ Man!"
Barnaby exhaled in a screamed whisper, trying

not to panic over the fact that the man who was
supposed to finally make them feel better was
not going to be able to help them tonight, they
might die and never be able to help them get
high again! That first wave of thoughts hit after
their reflexes had already kicked in dragging
Boxer's broken action figure body to the car to
drive them to the hospital, intuitively knowing
that the paramedics would take over twenty
minutes to arrive. Boxer's head lolled. The
BOXER tattoo on the back of their neck and
THE DIRTY 5-30 on their right cheek were like
the high and low tide marks as their head swung
back and forth. Their mouth was foaming and
making a gurgling noise like waves. But this was
a nightmarish, schizophrenic surf, lost in a night
terror. And as Barnaby and Boxer raced to the
hospital in Barnaby's jalopy, Barnaby could only
think of two things. When were they getting
high next and man, how many drugs do they
have at that hospital?